the **Cocker Spaniel**

A guide to selection, care, nutrition,

upbringing, training, health, breeding

sports and play

Contents

Foreword

The book you are holding is a basic 'owners manual'
for everyone owning a Cocker Spaniel and also for
those who are considering buying a Cocker Spaniel.
What we have done in this book is to give the information to help the (future) owner of a Cocker Spaniel
look after his or her pet responsibly. Too many people
still buy a pet before really understanding what they're
about to get into.

This book goes into the broad history of the Cocker
Spaniel, the breed standard and some pros and cons of
buying a Cocker Spaniel. You will also find essential
information on feeding, initial training and an intro-
duction in reproduction. Finally we give attention to
(day-to-day) care, health and some breed-specific ailments.

Based on this information, you can buy a Cocker
Spaniel, having thought it through carefully, and keep
it as a pet in a responsible manner. Our advice, though,
is not just to leave it to this small book. A properly
brought-up and well-trained dog is more than just a
dog. Invest a little extra in a puppy training course or
an obedience course. There are also excellent books
available that go deeper into certain aspects than is
possible here.

About Pets

A Publication of About Pets.

Copyright © 2003
About Pets
co-publisher United Kingdom
Kingdom Books
PO9 5TL, England

ISBN 185279187X
First printing
September 2003

Original title: *de Engelse Cocker spaniël*
© 2000 - 2002 Welzo Media Productions bv,
About Pets,
Warffum, the Netherlands
http://www.aboutpets.info

Photos:
Rob Doolaard, Helga Hosten,
Fam. De Mes, Fam. Van Soelen, Riet Kamstra,
Agnes Bootsma, Rob Dekker, Y. de Vries,
W. Hasselmeijer, L. van Melle,
H. van Wessem and Astrid Verweij

Printed in Italy

In general

The Cocker Spaniel described in this book is the "English Cocker Spaniel". Its official breed name distinguishes the breed from the American Cocker Spaniel, which is regarded as a separate and largely different breed.

The Cocker Spaniel is well known as a very popular pet. Anyone looking into its dark, affectionate and intelligent eyes immediately knows why this is the case. It has that "melting expression", a gaze that will truly melt the heart. Not only is the English Cocker mild-natured, intelligent and lively, but it looks beautiful too. Its coat is soft, glossy and springy and can be in a wide variety of colours.

The Cocker is a lively and merry character that likes company. Its happiness is characterised by the breed's typical feature, its ever-wagging tail. Originally a hunting dog, the Cocker Spaniel is not one for laying around. It is an athlete that will only be at its best if it's always in motion.

Origin
Without doubt, the English Cocker Spaniel is one of the world's oldest breeds, and in all probability has its origins on the European mainland. Coins have been discovered with the image of Alexander the Great hunting together with big greyhounds and smaller longhaired dogs of the spaniel variety. One assumes that western Europeans (among them Celts), on the move before the Romans and later the Norman invasion, brought the spaniel with them to the British Isles. The adulteration of these peoples' languages finally led to the name 'spaniel' derived from the French 'epagneul' and the Spanish 'espagnol'. This would imply that the early origins of this breed are to be found in Spain.

The first documented appearance of the spaniel name dates from 948. Among the laws of the Welsh king, Howell the Good, the values of the various breeds of dog are laid down in the paragraph 'The Worth of Dogs'. The value of the 'King's Spaniel' is set at one pound, an amount that in those days would buy a number of goats, geese, slaves or even a wife. Chaucer (1328-1400) describes the spaniel in one of his works, albeit in a less positive manner – he found the dog too friendly by nature. Around 1570, in his famous 'Treatise of Englishe Dogges', Dr. J. Caius, the physician to the court of Elizabeth I and founder of Caius College, Cambridge, described all the spaniels as being white with red, or white with black. He also noted their friendly character and their constantly wagging tail.

words they drove it out of cover. Before the invention of the hunting rifle, the hunters then set their falcons loose on the game. From this last group of spaniels later came driving dogs. The name 'Cocker Spaniel' first appears around 1800. These dogs were excellent assistants when hunting for woodcock, and have their name as a result.

Orange

During the nineteenth century, spaniels in Great Britain were classified into large spaniels ('Fields') and smaller spaniels ('Cockers'). The minor differences between the two groups made their weight the decisive factor. Dogs heavier than 25 pounds were Fields, anything lighter were Cockers. In the second half of the nineteenth century, British breeders began to specifically breed today's English Cocker Spaniel.

Development

Spaniels have been used for centuries as versatile hunting dogs. Dr. Caius distinguished in his work between water and land spaniels. The land spaniels were used in three different ways when hunting birds. The 'creeping' spaniels were used when netting birds. They lay in front of the bird and the hunters threw their nets over bird and dogs. The setting spaniels captured the game and also allowed themselves to be caught under the net. The springing spaniels 'sprang' the game, in other

Blue

The English Spaniel Club was founded in 1885. The weight of the dog remained decisive for its 'breed' until 1901. In 1902, the breed standard for the Cocker Spaniel was officially approved by the British kennel club.

Breed standard

A standard has been developed for all breeds recognised by the Kennel Club for the UK (and in Europe by the F.C.I. - the umbrella organisation for Western European kennel clubs). Officially approved kennel clubs in the member countries provide a translation. This standard provides a guideline for breeders and inspectors. It is something of an ideal that dogs of the breed must strive to match. With some breeds, dogs are already bred that match the ideal. Other breeds have a long

way to go. There is a list of defects for each breed. These can be serious defects that disqualify the dog, and it will be excluded from breding. Permitted defects are not serious, but do cost points in a show.

The UK Kennel Club breed standard for the English Cocker Spaniel

General Appearance

Merry, sturdy, sporting; well balanced; compact; measuring approximately same from withers to ground as from withers to root of tail.

Characteristics

Merry nature with ever-wagging tail shows a typical bustling movement particularly when following scent, fearless for heavy cover.

Nine spaniel breeds. From left to right: English Cocker Spaniel, American Cocker and Sussex (on the bench), Clumber, Irish Water, Welsh Springer, Field, English Springer and the American Water Spaniel

Temperament

Gentle and affectionate, yet full of life and exuberance.

Head and Skull

Square muzzle, with distinct stop set midway between tip of nose and occiput. Skull well developed, cleanly chiselled neither too fine nor too coarse. Cheek bones not prominent. Nose sufficiently wide for acute scenting power.

Eyes

Full but not prominent. Dark brown or brown, never light, but in the case of liver, liver roan, and liver and white, dark hazel to harmonise with coat; with expression of intelligence and gentleness but wide awake, bright and merry, rims tight.

Ears

Lobular, set low on a level with eyes. Fine leathers extending to nose tip. Well clothed with long straight silky hair.

Mouth

Jaws strong with a perfect, regular and complete scissor bite. i.e. upper teeth closely overlapping lower teeth and set square to the jaws.

Neck

Moderate in length, muscular. Set neatly into a fine sloping shoulders. Clean throat.

Forequarters

Shoulders sloping and fine. Legs well boned, straight, sufficiently short for concentrated power. Not too short to interfere with tremen-

dous exertions expected from this grand, sporting dog.

Body
Strong, compact. Chest well developed and brisket deep, neither too wide nor too narrow in front. Ribs well sprung. Loin short, wide with firm. level topline gently sloping downwards to tail from the end of loin to the set on the tail.

Hindquarters
Wide, well rounded, very muscular. Legs well boned, good bend of stifle, short below hock allowing for plenty of drive.

Feet
Firm, thickly padded, cat-like.

Tail
Set on slightly lower than line of back. Must be merry in action and carried level, never cocked up. Customarily docked.
Docked : Never too short to hide, nor too long to interfere with the incessant merry action when working.
Undocked : Slightly curved, of moderate length, proportionate to size of body, giving an overall balanced appearance; ideally not reaching below the hock. Strong at the root and tapering to a fine tip; well feathered in keeping with the coat. Lively in action, carried on a plane not higher than the level of the back and never so low as to indicate timidity.

Gait / Movement
True through action with great drive covering ground well.

Coat
Flat, silky in texture, never wiry or wavy, not profuse and never curly. Well feathered forelegs, body and hind legs above hocks.

Colour
Various. In self colours no white allowed except on chest.

Size
Height approximately -
Dogs 39-41 cms (15.5-16 ins) -
Bitches 38-39 cms (15-15.5 ins).
Weight approximately 28-32 lbs.

Faults
Any departure from the foregoing points should be considered a fault and the seriousness with which the fault should be regarded should be in exact proportion to its degree.

Breed standard by courtesy of the Kennel Club of Great Britain

A docked tail

Undocked tail

Buying a Cocker Spaniel

Once you've made that properly considered decision to buy a dog, there are several options. Should it be a puppy, an adult dog, or even an older dog? Should it be a bitch or dog, a pedigree dog or a cross?

Of course, the question also comes up as to where to buy your dog - from a private person, a reliable breeder or an animal shelter? For you and the animal, it's vital to get these questions sorted out in advance. You want a dog that will fit your circumstances properly. With a puppy, you get a playful energetic housemate that will easily adapt to a new environment. If you want something quieter, an older dog is a good choice.

Pros and cons of the Cocker Spaniel
The Cocker is a cheerful, happy dog. Its constantly wagging tail shows that it wants to join in everything. When you get up it, stands waiting. It loves a diversion and is inquisitive through and through. A Cocker Spaniel loves

life and is always an optimist. This affectionate dog will share happiness in the family, but your darker moods will also affect it; it feels the mood exactly. With its pretty appearance and that melting look, the Cocker has been able to seduce many; it's a real charmer.

However pretty, this breed's coat does need a lot of intensive groming. Your Cocker must be thoroughly brushed and combed three to four times a week, and needs to be trimmed every couple of months.

As charming as it is, the Cocker loves action. Originally a hunting dog, it is athletic and energetic. You're not done with once around the block; a Cocker Spaniel must work off its energy every day with a run in the open. If it gets that opportunity, you'll have no problems with it at home.

In general, there is a slight difference in character between the single or 'self' coloured (black and red) and the variegated Cocker. Self-coloured dogs are often more independent and need a stricter and more consistent up-bringing than the variegated variety.

Male or female?

Whether you choose a male or a female puppy, or an adult dog or bitch, is an entirely personal decision. A male typically needs more leadership because he tends to be more dominant in nature. He will try to play boss over other dogs and, if he gets the chance, over people too. In the wild, the most dominant dog (or wolf) is always the leader of the pack. In many cases this is a male. A bitch is much more focussed on her master, she sees him as the pack leader.

A puppy test is good for defining the kind of character a young dog will develop. During a test one usually sees that a dog is more dominant than a bitch. You can often quickly recognise the bossy, the adventurous and the cautious characters. So visit the litter a couple of times early on. Try to pick a puppy that suits your own personality. A dominant dog, for instance, needs a strong hand. It

will often try to see how far it can go. You must regularly make it clear who's the boss, and that it must obey all the members of the family.

When bitches are sexually mature, they will go into season. On average, a bitch is in season twice a year for about two or three weeks. This is the fertile period when she can become pregnant. Particularly in the second half of her season, she will want to go looking for a dog to mate with. A male dog will show more masculine traits once he is sexually mature. He will make sure other dogs know what territory is his by urinating as often as possible in as many places as he can. He is also difficult to restrain if there's a bitch in season nearby. As far as normal care is concerned there is little difference between a dog and a bitch.

Puppy or adult?

After you've made the decision for a male or female, the next question comes up. Should it be a puppy or an adult dog? Your household circumstances usually play a major role here.

Of course, it's great having a sweet little puppy in the house, but bringing up a young dog requires a lot of time. In the first year of its life it learns more than during the rest of its life. This is the period when the foundations are laid for elementary matters

Puppy

... or a adult?

such as house-training, obedience and social behaviour. You must reckon with the fact that your puppy will keep you busy for a couple of hours a day, certainly in the first few months. You won't need so much time with a grown dog. It has already been brought up, but this doesn't mean it won't need correcting from time to time.

A puppy will no doubt leave a trail of destruction in its wake for the first few months. With a little bad luck, this will cost you a number of rolls of wallpaper, some good shoes and a few socks. In the worst case you'll be left with some chewed furniture. Some puppies even manage to tear curtains from their rails. With good upbringing this 'vandalism' will quickly disappear, but you won't have to worry about this if you get an older dog.

The greatest advantage of a puppy, of course, is that you can bring it up your own way. And the upbringing a dog gets (or doesn't get) is a major influence on its whole character. Finally, financial aspects may play a role in your choice. A puppy is generally (much) more expensive than an adult dog, not only in purchase price but also in 'maintenance'. A puppy needs to go to the vet's more often for the necessary vaccinations and check-ups. Overall, bringing up a puppy involves a good deal of energy, time and money, but you have its upbringing in your own hands. An

adult dog costs less money and time, but its character is already formed. You should also try to find out about the background of an adult dog. Its previous owner may have formed its character in somewhat less positive ways.

Two dogs?

Having two or more dogs in the house is not just nice for us, but also for the animals themselves. Dogs get a lot of pleasure from their own company. After all, they are pack animals.

If you're sure that you want two young dogs, it's best not to buy them at the same time. Bringing a dog up and establishing the bond between dog and master takes time, and you need to give a lot of attention to your dog in this phase. Having two puppies in the house means you have to divide your attention between them. Apart from that, there's a danger that they will focus on one another rather than on their master. Buy the second pup when the first is (almost) an adult.

Two adult dogs can happily be brought into the home together, as long as they're used to each other. If this is not the case, then they have to go through that process. This is usually best achieved by letting them get to know each other on neutral territory. This prevents fights for territory. On neutral territory, perhaps an acquaintance's garden where neither dog has been before, both dogs are basically equal. Once they've got to know each other, you can take them both home, and they can sort out the hierarchy there amongst themselves. In any event, don't get involved in trying to 'arbitrate'. That is human, but for the dog that's at the top of the pecking order it's like having its position undone. It will only make the dog more dominant in behaviour, with all the consequences. Once the hierarchy is established, most dogs can get along fine together.

Getting a puppy when the first dog is somewhat older often has a positive effect on the older dog. The influence of the puppy almost seems to give it a second child-

hood. The older dog, if it's been well brought up, can help with the up-bringing of the puppy. Young dogs like to imitate the behaviour of their elders. Don't forget to give both dogs the same amount of attention. Take both out alone at least once per day during the first eighteen months. Give the older dog enough opportunity to get some peace and quiet. It won't want an enthusiastic youngster running around under its feet all the time. Moreover, a puppy needs plenty of sleep and may have to have the brakes put on it once in a while.

The combination of a male and female needs special attention and it's good advice to get a second dog of the same sex. This will avoid a lot of problems.

Sterilisation and castration is, of course, one solution, but it's a final one. A sterilised or castrated animal can never reproduce.

A dog and children

Dogs and children are a great combination. They can play together and get great pleasure out of each other's company. Moreover, children need to learn how to handle living beings; they develop respect and a sense of responsibility by caring for a dog (or other pets). However sweet a dog is, children must understand that it is an animal and not a toy. A dog isn't comfortable when it's being messed around with. It can become frightened, timid and even aggressive. So make it clear what a dog likes and what it doesn't.

Look for ways the child can play with the dog, perhaps a game of hide and seek where the child hides and the dog has to find it. Even a simple tennis ball can give enormous pleasure. Children must learn to leave a dog in peace when it doesn't want to play any more. The dog must also have its own place where it's not disturbed. Have children help with your dog's care as much as possible. A strong bond will be the result.

The arrival of a baby also means changes in the life of a dog. Before the birth you can help get the dog acquainted with the new situation. Let it sniff at the new things in the house and it will quickly accept them. When the baby has arrived involve the dog

as much as possible in day-by-day events, but make sure it gets plenty of attention too. NEVER leave a dog alone with young children. Crawling infants sometimes make unexpected movements, which can easily frighten a dog. And infants are hugely curious, and may try to find out whether the tail is really fastened to the dog, or whether its eyes come out, just like they do with their cuddly toys. But a dog is a dog and it will defend itself when it feels threatened.

Where to buy

There are various ways of acquiring a dog. The decision for a puppy or an adult dog will also define for the most part where to buy your dog.

If it's to be a puppy, then you need to find a breeder with a litter. If you chose a popular breed, like the English Cocker Spaniel, there is choice enough. But you may also face the problem that there are so many puppies on sale that have only been bred for profit's sake. You can see how many puppies are for sale by looking in the regional newspaper every Saturday. Some of these dogs have a pedigree, but many don't. These breeders often don't watch out for breed-specific illnesses and inbreeding; puppies are separated from their mother as fast as possible and are thus insufficiently socialised. Never buy a puppy that is too young, or whose mother you weren't able to see.

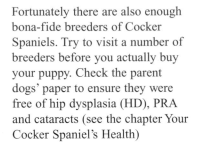

Fortunately there are also enough bona-fide breeders of Cocker Spaniels. Try to visit a number of breeders before you actually buy your puppy. Check the parent dogs' paper to ensure they were free of hip dysplasia (HD), PRA and cataracts (see the chapter Your Cocker Spaniel's Health)

Also ask if the breeder is prepared to help you after you've bought your puppy, and to help you find solutions for any problems that may come up.

Finally, you should realise that a pedigree is nothing more or less than evidence of descent. Most kennel clubs also award pedigrees to the offspring of dogs suffering from hereditary conditions, or dogs that have never been checked for them. A pedigree therefore says nothing about the parent dogs' health.

If you're looking for an adult dog, you can also contact the breed association, who often help place adult dogs that can no longer be kept by their owners because of personal circumstances (impulse buying, moving home, divorce etc.).

Things to watch out for

Buying a puppy is no simple matter. You must pay attention to the following:
• Never buy a puppy on impulse, even if it is love at first sight. A dog is a living being that will

Ten golden puppy rules

1. Walk your puppy in doses followed by one hour play, a feed and then three hours sleep.
2. Don't let your puppy run endlessly after a ball or stick.
3. Don't let your puppy romp wildly with large, heavy dogs.
4. Never let your puppy play on a full tummy.
5. Don't give your puppy anything to drink straight after a meal.
6. Don't let your puppy walk up and down steps for the first year. Be careful with shiny floors.
7. Don't add supplements to ready-made food.
8. Watch out for your puppy's weight. Being overweight can lead to bone abnormalities.
9. Give your puppy a quiet place to sleep.
10. Pick your puppy up carefully, one hand under its chest, the other under its hindquarters

need care and attention over a long period. It is not a toy that you can put away when you're finished with it.

- Take a good look at the mother. Is she calm, nervous, aggressive, well cared-for or neglected? The behaviour and condition of the mother is not only a sign of the quality of the breeder, but also of the puppy you're about to buy.
- Avoid buying a puppy whose mother has been kept only in a kennel. A young dog needs as many different impressions as possible in its first few months, including living in a family group. It gets used to people and possibly other pets. Kennel dogs miss these experiences and are inadequately socialised.
- Always ask to see the parents' papers (vaccination certificates, pedigrees, official reports on health examinations).
- Never buy a puppy younger than eight weeks.
- Put all agreements with the breeder in writing. A model agreement is available from the Kennel Club.

Travelling with your Cocker Spaniel

There are a few things to think about before travelling with your dog. While one dog may enjoy travelling, another may hate it.

You may like holidays in far-away places, but it's questionable whether your dog will enjoy them as much.

That very first trip

The first trip of a puppy's life is also the most nerve-wracking. This is the trip from the breeder's to its new home. If you can, pick up your puppy in the early morning. Then it will have plenty of time to get used to its new surroundings. Ask the breeder not to feed the puppy that day. The young animal will be overwhelmed by all kinds of new experiences. Firstly, it's away from its mother; it's in a small room (the car) with all its different smells, noises and strange people. So there's a big chance that the puppy will be car-sick this first time, with the annoying consequence that it will remember travelling in the car as an unpleasant experience.

So it's important to make this first trip as pleasant as possible. When picking up a puppy, always take someone with you who can sit in the back seat with the puppy on his or her lap and talk to it calmly. If it's too warm for the puppy, a place on the floor at the feet of your companion is ideal. The pup will lie there relatively quietly and may even take a nap. Ask the breeder for a cloth or something else from the puppies basket or bed that carries a familiar scent. The puppy can lie on this in the car, and it will also help if it feels lonely during the first nights at home.

If the trip home is a long one, then stop for a break (once in a while). Let your puppy roam and sniff around (on the lead!), offer it a little drink and, if necessary, do its business. Do take care to lay an old towel in the car. It can happen that the puppy, in its nervousness, may urinate or be sick. It's also good advice to give a puppy positive experiences with car journeys. Make short trips to nice places where you can walk and play with it. It can be a real nuisance if your dog doesn't like travelling in a car. After all, once in a while you will have to take it to certain places, such as the vet's or to visit friends and acquaintances.

Taking your Cocker Spaniel on holiday

When making holiday plans, you also need to think about what you are going to do with your dog during that time. Are you taking it with you, putting it into kennels or leaving it with friends? In any event there are a number of things you need to do in good time. If you want to take your dog with you, you need to be sure in advance that it will be welcome at your holiday home, and what the rules there are. If you're going abroad it will need certain vaccinations and a health certificate, which normally need to be done four weeks before departure. You must also be sure that you've made all the arrangements necessary to bring your dog back home to the UK,

without it needing to go into quarantine under the rabies regulations. Your vet can give you the most recent information.

If your trip is to southern Europe, ask for a treatment against ticks (you can read more about this in the chapter on parasites).

Although dog-owners usually enjoy taking their dog on holiday, you must seriously ask yourself whether the dog feels that way too. Cocker Spaniels certainly don't always feel comfortable in a hot country. Days spent travelling in a car are also often not their preference, and some dogs suffer badly from car-sickness. There are good medicines for this, but it's questionable whether you're doing your dog a favour with them. If you do decide to take it with you, make regular stops at safe places during your journey, so that your dog can have a good run. Take plenty of fresh drinking water with you, as well as the food your dog is used to.

Don't leave your dog in the car standing in the sun. It can quickly be overcome by the heat, with even fatal consequences. If you can't avoid it, park the car in the shade if at all possible, and leave a window open for a little fresh air. Even if you've taken these precautions, never stay away long!

If you're travelling by plane or ship, make sure in good time that your dog can travel with you and what rules you need to observe. You will need some time to make all the arrangements. Maybe you decide not to take your dog with you, and you then need to find somewhere for it to stay.

Arrangements for a place in kennels need to be made well in advance, and there may be certain vaccinations required, which need to be given a minimum of one month before the stay.

If your dog can't be accommodated in the homes of relatives or friends, it might be possible to have an acquaintance stay in your house. This also needs to be arranged well in advance, as it may be difficult to find someone that can do this.

Always ensure that your dog can be traced should it run away or get lost while on holiday. A little tube

with your address or a tag with home and holiday address can prevent a lot of problems.

Moving home

Dogs generally become more attached to humans than to the house they live in. Moving home is usually not a problem for them. But it can be useful before moving to let the dog get to know its new home and the area around it.

If you can, leave your dog with relatives or friends (or in kennels) on the day of the move. The chance of it running away or getting lost is then practically non-existent. When your move is complete, you can pick your dog up and let it quietly get familiar with its new home and environment. Give it its own place in the house at once and it will quickly adapt. During the first week or so, always walk your dog on a lead because an animal can also get lost in new surroundings. Always take a different route so it quickly gets to know the neighbourhood.

Don't forget to get your new address and phone number engraved on the dog's tag. Send a change of address notice to chip or tattoo registration office. Dogs must sometimes be registered in a new community.

Nutrition, feeding your Cocker Spaniel

A dog will actually eat a lot more than just meat. In the wild it would eat its prey complete with skin and fur, including the bones, stomach, and the innards with their semi-digested vegetable material.

In this way the dog supplements its meat menu with the vitamins and minerals it needs. This is also the basis for feeding a domestic dog.

Ready-made foods

It's not easy for a layman to put together a complete menu for a dog, that includes all the necessary proteins, fats, vitamins and minerals in just the right proportions and quantities. Meat alone is certainly not a complete meal for a dog. It contains too little calcium. A calcium deficiency over time will lead to bone defects, and for a fast-growing puppy this can lead to serious skeletal deformities.

If you mix its food yourself, you can easily give your dog too much in terms of vitamins and minerals, which can also be bad for your dog's health. You can avoid these problems by giving it ready-made food of a good brand. These products are well-balanced and contain everything your dog needs. Supplements such as vitamin preparations are superfluous. The amount of food your dog needs depends on its weight and activity level. You can find guidelines on the packaging. Split the food into two meals per day if possible, and always ensure there's a bowl of fresh drinking water next to its food.

Give your dog the time to digest its food, don't let it outside straight after a meal. A dog should also never play on a full stomach. This can cause stomach torsion, (the stomach turning over), which can be fatal for your dog.

Because the nutritional needs of a dog depend, among other things, on its age and way of life, there are many different types of dog food available. There are "light" foods for less active dogs, "energy" foods for working dogs and "senior" foods for the older dog.

Canned foods, mixer and dry foods

Ready-made foods available at pet shops or in the supermarket can roughly be split into canned food, mixer and dry food. Whichever form you choose, ensure that it's a complete food with all the necessary ingredients. You can see this on the packaging.

Most dogs love canned food. Although the better brands are composed well, they do have one disadvantage: they are soft. A dog fed only on canned food will sooner or later have problems with its teeth (plaque, paradontosis). Besides canned food, give your dog hard foods at certain times or a dog chew, such as Nylabone Healthy Edibles.

Mixer is a food consisting of chunks, dried vegetables and grains. Almost all moisture has been extracted. The advantages of mixer are that it is light and keeps well. You add a certain amount of water and the meal is ready. A disadvantage is that it must definitely not be fed without water. Without the extra fluid, mixer will absorb the fluids present in the stomach, with serious results. Should your dog manage to get at the bag and enjoy its contents, you must immediately give it plenty to drink.

Dry chunks have also had the moisture extracted but not as much as mixer. The advantage of dry foods is that they are hard, forcing the dog to use its jaws, removing plaque and massaging the gums.

Dog chew products

Of course, once in a while you want to spoil your dog with something extra. Don't give it pieces of cheese or sausage as these contain too much salt and fat. There are various products available that a

Gerookte botten

Munchi sticks

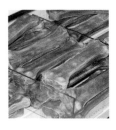

Kauwkluiven

dog will find delicious and which are also healthy, especially for its teeth, such as Nylabone. You'll find a large range of varying quality in the pet shop.

The butcher's left-overs

The bones of slaughtered animals have traditionally been given to the dog and dogs love them, but they are not without risks. Pork and poultry bones are too weak. They can splinter and cause serious injury to the intestines. Beef bones are more suitable, but they must first be cooked to kill off dangerous bacteria.

Pet shops carry a range of smoked, cooked and dried abattoir residue, such as pigs' ears, bull penis, tripe sticks, oxtails, gullet, dried muscle meat, and hoof chews.

Fresh meat

If you do want to give your dog fresh meat occasionally, never give it raw, but always boiled or roasted. Raw (or not fully cooked) pork or chicken can contain life-threatening bacteria. Chicken can be contaminated by the notorious salmonella bacteria, while pork can carry the Aujeszky virus. This disease is incurable and will quickly lead to the death of your pet.

Buffalo or cowhide chews

Dog chews are mostly made of beef or buffalo hide. Chews are usually knotted or pressed hide and can come in the form of little shoes, twisted sticks, lollies, balls and various other shapes; nice to look at and a nice change.

Munchy sticks

Munchy sticks are green, yellow, red or brown coloured sticks of various thicknesses. They consist of ground buffalo hide with a number of often undefined additives. The composition and quality of these between-meal treats is not always clear. Some are fine, but there have also been sticks found to contain high levels of cardboard and even paint residues. Choose a product whose ingredients are clearly described.

Overweight?

Recent investigations have shown that many dogs are overweight. A dog usually gets too fat because of over-feeding and lack of exercise. Use of medicines or a disease is rarely the cause. Dogs that get too fat are often given too much food or treats between meals. Gluttony or boredom can also be a cause, and a dog often puts on weight following castration or sterilisation. Due to changes in hormone levels, it becomes less active and consumes less energy. Finally, simply too little exercise alone can lead to a dog becoming overweight.

You can use the following rule of thumb to check whether your dog is overweight: you should be able to feel its ribs, but not see them. If you can't feel its ribs then your

dog is much too fat. Overweight dogs live a passive life, they play too little and tire quickly. They also suffer from all kinds of medical problems (problems in joints and heart conditions). They usually die younger too.

So it's important to make sure your dog doesn't get too fat. Always follow the guidelines on food packaging. Adapt them if your dog is less active or gets lots of snacks. Try to make sure your dog gets plenty of exercise by playing and running with it as much as you can. If your dog starts to show signs of putting on weight you can switch to a low-calorie food. If it's really too fat and reducing its food quantity doesn't help, then a special diet is the only solution.

Caring for your Cocker Spaniel

Good (daily) care is extremely important for your dog. A well-cared for dog is less likely to become ill.

Caring for your dog is not only necessary but also a pleasure. Master and dog are giving each other some attention, and it's an excellent opportunity for a game and a cuddle.

The coat

Caring for your dog's coat involves regular brushing and combing, together with checking for parasites such as fleas. How often a dog needs to be brushed and combed depends on the length of its coat. The sumptuous coat of an English Cocker Spaniel needs intensive grooming. Brushing not only stimulates blood circulation under the skin but lends the silky coat a fine gloss. Your Cocker needs a good brushing three to four times a week. Proper brushing is something that needs to be learned. You can ask the breeder to show you how this should be done. At young dog events organised by the breed association, there will be experienced trimmers who can help you.

Use the right equipment for grooming. Get your puppy used to being brushed and everything else that needs to be done from an early age. Teach it that it will always be groomed on a table. That relieves your back; you can get everywhere and your dog will be used to it when the time comes for its first trim. Also get it used to lying on its back and side during brushing. That way, you won't need to miss anything and it will quickly become accustomed to lying in those positions.

Brushes must not be too hard for the Cocker's silky coat, otherwise they may damage or break its hairs. Using a soft brush, first rub over the dogs neck, shoulders, upper and sides of the back, the sides of the paws and the root of the tail. This brush should consist of an elongated block of rubber with blunt springy points. This massage stimulates blood circulation and removes loose (mostly white) hairs from the coat.

Then brush the entire dog with a universal brush or comb. Always brush from head to tail with the direction of the coat. The best sequence is ears, chest, underside of front paws, armpits, groin and rear paws. Give special attention to the fur inside the ears. Thick hair can stop fresh air getting into the ears, causing infections.

You can then comb your dog with a fine steel comb, whereby you remove as much dead hair and fluff as possible. Comb down to the skin, otherwise the undercoat will eventually become matted. Finally, brush it one more time with a stiff hairbrush. Remove any tangles you find during grooming immediately.

Tangles occur above all in wet weather and if your dog often likes to run through high grass or bushes. Small tangles frequently found behind the ears, in the armpits and groin should be carefully plucked out using your fingers or a coarse comb. Then comb them through with a fine comb. Be very careful because dogs find this plucking very painful. If tangles are too big or too deep to pluck out, cut them out with a sharp pair of scissors. Use scissors with blunt points and keep the points away from the dog. After removing tangles, comb the coat thoroughly with a fine comb until you're sure you've removed all tangles from your dog's coat.

Your Cocker only needs a bath when it's really necessary. Make sure its coat is tangle-free before washing. Washing the paws and belly with lukewarm water is usually sufficient. In other cases, use a good non-alkaline dog or baby shampoo, which won't remove the natural fats in the skin. You may want to use a little conditioner to make the coat softer in structure. Rinse your dog thoroughly to prevent residues of soap, which might cause irritation.

Rub your Cocker thoroughly dry and let it dry completely in a warm, draught-free room. You can even use a hair-dryer. Never let a wet dog outdoors; dogs can catch colds too!

A vet can prescribe special medicinal shampoos for some skin conditions. Always follow the instructions to the letter. Good flea prevention is highly important

- Fine steel comb

- Coarse steel comb

- Universal brush

- Stiff-haired brush

- Rubber massage brush

- Thinning shears, one-sided

- Straight scissors with rounded tips

- Rubber thimble

- Magnesium block or trimming chalk

to avoid skin and coat problems. Fleas must be treated not only on the dog itself but also in its surroundings (see the chapter on parasites). Coat problems can also occur due to an allergy to certain food substances. In such cases, a vet can prescribe a hypo-allergenic diet.

Trimming

One Cocker will have a smooth coat that is easy to maintain; another may have a thick, woolly coat that needs to be plucked and brushed more often. The woolly puppy coat should be plucked completely at the moment hairs start falling out. On average, full-grown red Cocker Spaniels will need trimming two to three times per year, and black Cockers and blue roans three to four times. It depends on the speed at which their hair grows and the normal grooming that you apply. The dog is 'ready for plucking' when hair starts falling out by itself.

The goal of trimming is, among other things, to remove dead hair and to thin out superfluous hair to accentuate the dog's pretty form as far as possible. Good trimming is an art form that needs to be learnt. Take a good look at how Cockers are trimmed at dog shows. With a lot of patience and good instruction, you can do this yourself. Roughen your fingertips before trimming with a magnesium block (available in sports stores). You can

also use rubber thimbles that are often used to count money (available in stationery shops).

Plucking always takes place in the direction of the hair roots. If you pluck in the other direction, you will hurt your dog. Hold the dog's skin as tight as possible and, at the same time, pluck out small bunches of hair. Start by plucking out all the long hair on the dog's skull and around the ear roots (just above the ears). This will give your Cocker a nice smooth head and well-pronounced ears. You might want to thin out the sides at the ends of the cheekbones. Never use scissors to clip away the long hairs on the head! The hair that then regrows is often different in structure, grows even faster and, above all, is difficult to pluck.

If you lift the ear, you will see long hairs surrounding the ear opening. Trim these hairs away evenly using thinning shears or normal sharp scissors. This prevents 'sweating' in the ears, which can cause infections. This will also help you clean your dog's ears if necessary. Eyebrows, whiskers and all the long hair around the mouth can be clipped away with normal scissors. Pay special attention to the hair around the sides of the lips (lip eczema!).

You must pluck away long hairs in the neck and shoulder area with your fingers. The hair on the ribs may stand out and this must also be removed. As a check, look down on the dog from above. No hair should stick out to the side.

Don't trim the belly hair away! If it is too long and downy, trim it back a little. Pluck the long hair on the front of the forepaws away with your fingers, the 'feathering' must not be plucked or trimmed away, at most trimmed back a little. The feathering must not touch the ground. You can ensure this by combing it downwards. Hairs that protrude from the paws can then be clipped away. Hairs that stick out to the side of the forepaws need to be plucked away.

The paws should be small and arched. Regular trimming makes your dog look well cared for and, moreover, it will bring less dirt into the house. Trim away and shape all protruding hairs using thinning shears to form a nicely shaped paw. Clip back hairs on the underside of the paws to the same level as the soles. Don't remove the hair between the toes! Your dog should have nice 'cats' feet' and not spread out toes.

Try to get the croup (end of the back and beginning of the tail) and the sides of the hindlegs are smooth as possible by brushing, combing and plucking. Be careful with the transition from back to croup and tail. Blue roans, especially, often have excess hair growth

here. Never clip or pluck away the hairs on the inside of the hindlegs. You may want to trim them back a little, but they should always be left somewhat longer than the knee joint. The underside of the hind legs is called the 'heel'. Thin out or clip hairs from the rear of the hindlegs from the heel to the ground.

Clip away the plumage on the tail. On top of the tail, pluck as much as possible; on the underside of the tail thin out and shorten the hair with the thinning shears. If your Cocker has a lot of fur around the anus, thin this out carefully.

The hairs between the rear legs are called the 'breech', and the breech is the Cocker's pride. If it is very thick and full, thin it out a little. Trim back any long hairs that almost reach the ground, but never shorter than just past the heel.

Teeth

A dog must be able to eat properly to stay in good condition, so it needs healthy teeth. Check its teeth regularly. Get in touch with your vet if you suspect that all is not well. Regular feeds of hard dry food can help keep your dogs teeth clean and healthy. There are special dog chews, such as Nylabone, on the market that help prevent plaque and help keep the animal's breath fresh.

What really helps is regular tooth-brushing. You can use special tooth-brushes for dogs, but a finger wrapped in a small piece of gauze will also do the job. Get your dog used to having its teeth cleaned at an early age and you won't have problems.

You can even teach an older dog to have its teeth cleaned. With a dog chew as a reward it will certainly be happy.

Nails

On a dog that regularly walks on hard surfaces, its nails usually grind themselves down. In this case there's no need to clip their nails. But it wouldn't do any harm to check their length now and again, especially on dogs that don't get out on the streets often. Using a piece of paper, you can easily see whether its nails are too long. If you can push the paper between the nail and the ground when the dog is standing, then the nail is the right length.

Nails that are too long can bother a dog. It can injure itself when scratching, so they must be kept trimmed. You can buy special nail clippers in pet shops. Be careful not to clip back too far as you

could damage the skin around the nail, which can bleed profusely. If you feel unsure, have this necessary task done by a vet or an professional groomer.

You can also file your dog's nails back. This is best done with a foot rasp that you can buy at a chemist's. Your dog will need to get used to the feeling, but this is a safe method as you can see exactly how far you can go.

Eyes

A dog's eyes should be cleaned regularly. Discharge gets into the corners of the eye. You can easily remove them by wiping them downward with your thumb. If you don't like doing that, use a piece of tissue or toilet paper.

Keeping your dog's eyes clean will take only a few seconds a day, so do it every day. If the discharge becomes yellow this could point to an irritation or infection. Eye drops (from your vet) will quickly solve this problem.

Ears

The ears are often forgotten when caring for dogs, but they must be checked at least once a week. If your dog's ears are very dirty or show too much wax, you must clean them. This should preferably be done with a clean cotton cloth, moistened with lukewarm water or baby oil. Cotton wool is not suitable due to the fluff it can

leave behind. NEVER penetrate the ear canal with an object. If you do neglect cleaning your dog's ears there's a substantial risk of infection. A dog that is constantly scratching at its ears might be suffering from dirty ears, an ear infection or ear mites, making a visit to the vet essential.

Lips

Lip eczema on the lower lip (side of snout) is common on Cocker Spaniels. This eczema is caused by bacteria from food remnants lodged in the folds of the skin. Skin eczema can give off a particularly unpleasant smell, which can be detected yards away. This condition must be treated with a special lotion.

You can reduce the risk of lip eczema to a minimum by cleaning your dog's lips thoroughly after each feed (for example with a betadine-iodine solution) and then drying them. Also keep the hair around the snout short. Don't clean food bowls with washing-up liquid, but only with hot water. A correction of the lip fold is often regarded as a definite solution. In this surgical procedure, the lip is tightened so that the fold disappears. However, this method is not always successful.

Bringing up your Cocker Spaniel

It is very important that your dog is properly brought up and is obedient. Not only will this bring you more pleasure, but it's also nicer for your environment.

A puppy can learn what it may and may not do by playing. Rewards and consistency are important tools in bringing up a dog. Reward it with your voice, a stroke or something tasty and it will quickly learn to obey. A puppy-training course can also help you along the way.

(Dis)obedience

A dog that won't obey you is not just a problem for you, but also for your surroundings. It's therefore important to avoid unwanted behaviour. In fact, this is what training your dog is all about, so get started early. 'Start 'em young!' applies to dogs too. An untrained dog is not just a nuisance, but can also cause dangerous situations, running into the road, chasing joggers or jumping at

people. A dog must be trained out of this undesirable behaviour as quickly as possible. The longer you let it go on, the more difficult it will become to correct. The best thing to do is to attend a special obedience course. This won't only help to correct the dog's behaviour, but its owner also learns how to handle undesirable behaviour at home. A dog must not only obey its master during training, but at home too.

Always be consistent when training good behaviour and correcting annoying behaviour. This means a dog may always behave in a certain way, or must never behave that way. Reward it for good behaviour and never punish it after the fact for any wrongdoing. If your dog finally comes after you've been calling it a long time, then reward it. If you're angry because you had to wait so long, it may feel it's actually being punished for coming. It will probably not obey at all the next time for fear of punishment.

Try to take no notice of undesirable behaviour. Your dog will perceive your reaction (even a negative one) as a reward for this behaviour. If you need to correct the dog, then do this immediately. Use your voice or grip it by the scruff of its neck and push it to the ground. This is the way a mother dog calls her pups to order. Rewards for good behaviour are, by far, preferable to punishment; they always get a better result.

House-training

The very first training (and one of the most important) that a dog needs is house-training. The basis for good house-training is keeping a good eye on your puppy. If you pay attention, you will notice that it will sniff a long time and turns around a certain spot before doing its business there. Pick it up gently and place it outside, always at the same place. Reward it abundantly if it does its business there.

Another good moment for house-training is after eating or sleeping. A puppy often needs to do its business at these times. Let it relieve itself before playing with it, other-

wise it will forget to do so and you'll not reach your goal. For the first few days, take your puppy out for a walk just after it's eaten or woken up. It will quickly learn the meaning, especially if it's rewarded with a dog biscuit for a successful attempt. Of course, it's not always possible to go out after every snack or snooze. Lay newspapers at different spots in the house. Whenever the pup needs to do its business, place it on a newspaper. After some time it will start to look for a place itself. Then start to reduce the number of newspapers until there is just one left, at the front or back door. The puppy will learn to go to the door if it needs to relieve itself. Then you put it on the lead and go out with it. Finally you can remove the last newspaper. Your puppy is now house-trained.

One thing that certainly won't work is punishing an accident after the fact. A dog whose nose is rubbed in its urine or its droppings won't understand that at all. It will only get frightened of you. Rewarding works much better than punishment. An indoor kennel or cage can be a good tool in helping with house-training. A puppy won't foul its own nest, so a kennel can be a good solution for the night, or during periods in the day when you can't watch it. But a kennel must not become a prison where your dog is locked up day and night.

Basic obidience

Sit

The basic commands for an obedient dog are those for sit, lie down, come and stay. But a puppy should first learn its name. Use it as much as possible from the first day on followed by a friendly 'Come!' Reward it with your voice and a stroke when it comes to you. Your puppy will quickly recognise the intention and has now learned its first command in a playful manner. Don't be too harsh with a young puppy, and don't always punish it immediately if it doesn't always react in the right way. When you call your puppy to you in this way have it come right to you. You can teach a pup to sit by holding a piece of dog biscuit above his nose and then slowly moving it backwards. The puppy's head will also move backwards until its hind legs slowly go down. At that moment you clearly call 'Sit!' After a few attempts, it will quickly know this nice game. Use the 'Sit!' command before giving your dog its food, putting it on the lead, or before it's allowed to cross the road.

Teaching the command to lie down is similar. Instead of moving the piece of dog biscuit backwards, move it down vertically until your hand reaches the

ground and then forwards. The dog will also move its forepaws forwards and lie down on its own. At that moment clearly call 'Lie down!' This command is useful when you want a dog to be quiet.

Two people are needed for the 'Come!' command. One holds the dog back while the other runs away. After about fifteen metres, he stops and enthusiastically calls 'Come!' The other person now lets the dog go, and it should obey the command at once. Again you reward it abundantly. The 'Come!' command is useful in many situations and good for safety too.

A dog learns to stay from the sitting or lying position. While its sitting or lying down, you call the command: 'Stay!' and then step back one step. If the dog moves with you, quietly put it back in position, without displaying anger. If you do react angrily, you're actually punishing it for coming to you, and you'll only confuse your dog. It can't understand that coming is rewarded one time, and punished another. Once the dog stays nicely reward it abundantly. Practice this exercise with increasing distances (at first no more than one metre). The 'Stay!' command is useful when getting out of the car.

Down

Courses

Obedience courses to help you bring up your dog are available across the country. These courses are not just informative, but also fun for dog and master.

With a puppy, you can begin with a puppy course. This is designed to provide the basic training. A puppy that has attended such a course has learned about all kinds of things that will confront it in later life: other dogs, humans, traffic and what these mean. The puppy will also learn obedience and to follow a number of basic commands. Apart from all that, attention will be given to important subjects such as brushing, being alone, travelling in a car, and doing its business in the right places.

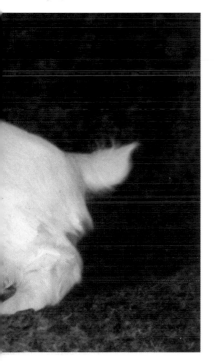

The next step after a puppy course is a course for young dogs. This course repeats the basic exercises and ensures that the growing dog doesn't learn bad habits. After this, the dog can move on to an obedience course for full-grown dogs. For more information on where to find courses in your area, contact your local kennel club. You can get its address from the Kennel Club of Great Britain in London. In some areas, the RSPCA organises obedience classes and your local branch may be able to give you information.

Play and toys

There are various ways to play with your dog, You can romp and run with it, but also play a number of games, such as retrieving, tug-of-war, hide-and-seek and catch. A tennis ball is ideal for retrieving, you can play tug-of-war with an old sock or a special tugging rope. Start with tug-of-war only when your dog is a year old. A puppy must first get its second teeth and then they need several months to strengthen. There's a real chance of your dog's teeth becoming deformed if you start too young. You can use almost anything for a game of hide-and-seek. A frisbee is ideal for catching games. Never use too small a ball for games. It can easily get lodged into the dog's throat.

Play is extremely important. Not only does it strengthen the bond

between dog and master, but it's also healthy for both. Make sure that you're the one that ends the game. Only stop when the dog has brought back the ball or frisbee, and make sure you always win the tug-of-war. This confirms your dominant position in the hierarchy. Use these toys only during play so that the dog doesn't forget their significance. When choosing a special dog toy, remember that dogs are hardly careful with them. So always buy toys of good quality that a dog can't easily destroy.

Be very careful with sticks and twigs. The latter, particularly, can easily splinter. A splinter of wood in your dog's throat or intestines can cause awful problems. Throwing sticks or twigs can also be dangerous. If they stick into the ground a dog can easily run into them with an open mouth.

If you would like to do more than just play games, you can now also play sports with your dog. For people who want to do more, there are various other sporting alternatives such as hunting trials, flyball and agility.

Aggression

Cocker Spaniels are normally practically never aggressive, however it can happen that it will be less friendly towards other animals or people. It's therefore a good idea to understand a little about the background of aggression in dogs. There are two different types of aggressive behaviour: The anxious-aggressive dog and the dominant-aggressive dog. An anxious-aggressive dog can be recognised by its pulled back ears and its low position. It will have pulled in its lips, showing its teeth. This dog is aggressive because it's very frightened and feels cornered. It would prefer to run away, but if it can't then it will bite to defend itself. It will grab its victim anywhere it can. The attack is usually brief and, as soon as the dog can see a way to escape, it's gone. In a confrontation with other dogs, it will normally turn out as the loser. It can become even more aggressive once it's realised that people or other dogs are afraid of it. This behaviour cannot be corrected just like that. First you have to try and understand what the dog is afraid of. Professional advice is a good idea here because the wrong approach can easily make the problem worse.

The dominant-aggressive dog's body language is different. Its ears stand up and its tail is raised and stiff. This dog will always go for its victim's arms, legs or throat. It is extremely self-assured and highly placed in the dog hierarchy. Its attack is a display of power rather than a consequence of fear. This dog needs to know who's boss. You must bring it up rigorously and with a strong hand.

An obedience course can help. A dog may also bite itself because it's in pain. This is a natural defensive reaction. In this case try to resolve the dog's fear as far as possible. Reward him for letting you get to the painful spot. Be careful, because a dog in pain may also bite its master! Muzzling it can help prevent problems if you have to do something that may be painful. Never punish a dog for this type of aggression!

Fear

The source of anxious behaviour can often be traced to the first weeks of a dog's life. A shortage of new experiences during this important phase (also called the 'socialisation phase') has great influence on its later behaviour. A dog that never encountered humans, other dogs or animals during the socialisation phase will be afraid of them later. This fear is common in dogs brought up in a barn or kennel, with almost no contact with humans. As we saw, fear can lead to aggressive behaviour, so it's important that a puppy gets as many new impressions as possible in the first weeks of its life. Take it with you into town in the car or on the bus, walk it down busy streets and allow it to have plenty of contact with people, other dogs and other animals.

It's a huge task to turn an anxious, poorly socialised dog into a real pet. It will probably take an enormous amount of attention, love, patience and energy to get such an animal used to everything around it. Reward it often and give it plenty of time to adapt and, over time, it will learn to trust you and become less anxious. Try not to force anything, because that will always have the reverse effect. Here too, an obedience course can help a lot. A dog can be especially afraid of strangers. Have visitors give it something tasty as a treat. Put a can of dog biscuits by the door so that your visitors can spoil your dog when they arrive. Here again, don't try to force anything. If the dog is still frightened, leave it in peace.

Dogs are often frightened in certain situations; well-known examples are thunderstorms and fireworks. In these cases try to ignore their anxious behaviour. If you react to a dog's whimpering and whining, it's the same as rewarding it. If you ignore its fear completely, your dog will quickly learn that nothing is wrong. You can speed up this 'learning process' by rewarding its positive behaviour.

Rewarding

Rewarding forms the basis for bringing up a dog. Rewarding good behaviour works far better than punishing bad behaviour and rewarding is also much more fun. Recently, the opinions on raising dogs have gradually changed. In the past the proper way to correct bad behaviour was regarded as a sharp pull on the lead. Today, experts view rewards as a positive incentive to get dogs to do what we expect of them. There are many ways to reward a dog. The usual ways are a stroke or a friendly word, even without a tasty treat to go with it. Of course, a piece of dog biscuit does wonders when you're training a puppy. Be sure you always have something delicious in your pocket to reward good behaviour. Another

form of reward is play. Whenever a dog notices you have a ball in your pocket, it won't go far from your side. As soon as you've finished playing, put the ball away. This way your dog will always do its best in exchange for a game.

Despite the emphasis you put on rewarding good behaviour, a dog can sometimes be a nuisance or disobedient. You must correct such behaviour immediately. Always be consistent: once 'no' always 'no'.

Barking

Dogs which bark too much and too often are a nuisance for their surroundings. A dog-owner may tolerate barking up to a point, but neighbours are often annoyed by the unnecessary noise. Don't encourage your puppy to bark and

yelp. Of course, it should be able to announce its presence, but if it goes on barking it must be called to order with a strict 'Quiet!'. If a puppy fails to obey, just hold its muzzle closed with your hand.

A dog will sometimes bark for long periods when left alone. It feels threatened and tries to get someone's attention by barking. There are special training pro-

grammes for this problem, where dogs learn that being alone is nothing to be afraid of, and that their master will always return.

You can practice this with your dog at home. Leave the room and come back in at once. Reward your dog if it stays quiet. Gradually increase the length of your absences and keep rewarding it as long as it remains quiet. Never punish the dog if it does bark or yelp. It will never understand punishment afterwards, and this will only make the problem worse. Never go back into the room as long as your dog is barking, as it will view this as a reward. You might want to make the dog feel more comfortable by switching the radio on for company during your absence. It will eventually learn that you always come back and the barking will reduce. If you don't get the required result, attend an obedience course.

Breeding

Dogs, and thus Cocker Spaniels, follow their instincts, and reproduction is one of nature's important processes.

For people who enjoy breeding dogs this is a positive circumstance. Those who simply want a cosy companion' however, do not need the regular adventures with females on heat and unrestrainable. Knowing a little about breeding in dogs will help you to understand why they behave the way they do, and the measures you need to take when this happens.

Liability

Breeding dogs is much more than simply 1+1= many. If you're planning to use your Cocker for breeding, be on your guard, otherwise the whole affair can turn into a financial drama because, under the law, a breeder is liable for the 'quality' of his puppies.

The breeder clubs place strict con-

ditions on animals used for breeding. They must be examined for possible congenital defects (see the chapter Your Cocker Spaniel's health). This is the breeder's first obligation, and if you breed a litter and sell the puppies without these checks having been made, you can be held liable by the new owners for any costs arising from any inherited defects. These (veterinary) costs can be enormous! So contact the breed association if you plan to breed a litter of Cockers.

The female in season

Bitches become sexually mature at about eight to twelve months. Then they go into season for the first time. They are 'in heat' for two to three weeks. During this period they discharge little drops of blood and they are very attractive to males. The bitch is fertile during the second half of her season, and will accept a male to mate. The best time for mating is then between the ninth and thirteenth day of her season. A female's first season is often shorter and less severe than those that follow. If you do want to use your female for breeding you must allow this first (and sometimes the second) season to pass. Most bitches go into season twice per year.

If you do plan to use your Cocker Spaniel for breeding in the future, then sterilization is not an option to prevent unwanted offspring. A temporary solution is a contraceptive injection, although this is controversial because of side effects such as womb infections.

Phantom pregnancy
A phantom pregnancy is a not an uncommon occurrence. The female behaves as if she has a litter. She takes all kinds of things to her basket and treats them like puppies. Her teats swell and sometimes milk is actually produced. The female will sometimes behave aggressively towards people or other animals, as if she is defending her young. Phantom pregnancies usually begin two months after a season and can last a number of weeks. If it happens to a bitch once, it will often then occur after every season. If she

suffers under it, sterilization is the best solution, because continual phantom pregnancies increase the risk of womb or teat conditions. In the short term a hormone treatment is worth trying, perhaps also homeopathic medicines. Camphor spirit can give relief when teats are heavily swollen, but rubbing the teats with ice or a cold cloth (moisten and freeze) can also help relieve the pain. Feed the female less than usual, and makes sure she gets enough attention and extra exercise.

Preparing to breed
If you do plan to breed a litter of puppies, you must first wait for your female to be physically and mentally full-grown. In any event you must let her first season pass. To mate a bitch, you need a male. You could simply let her out on the street and she will quickly return home pregnant.

But if you have a pure-bred Cocker bitch, then it certainly makes sense to mate her with the best possible candidate, even if she has no pedigree. Proceed with caution and think especially about the following: Accompanying a bitch through pregnancy, birth and the first eight to twelve weeks afterwards is a time consuming affair. Never use Cockers that have congenital defects for breeding, and this also applies to dogs without papers. The same goes for hyperactive, nervous and

shy dogs. If your Cocker Spaniel bitch does have a pedigree, then mate her with a dog that also has one. For more information, contact the breed association.

Pregnancy

It's often difficult to tell at first when a bitch is pregnant. Only after about four weeks can you feel the pups in her womb. She will now slowly get fatter and her behavior will usually change. Her teats will swell during the last few weeks of pregnancy. The average pregnancy lasts 63 days, and costs her a lot of energy. In the beginning she is fed her normal amount of food, but her nutritional needs increase in jumps during the second half of the pregnancy. Give her approximately fifteen percent more food each week from the fifth week on. The mother-to-be

needs extra energy and proteins during this phase of her pregnancy. During the last weeks you can give her a concentrated food, rich in energy, such as dry puppy food. Divide this into several small portions per day, because she can no longer deal with large portions of food. Towards the end of the pregnancy, her energy needs can easily be one-and-a-half times more than usual.

After about seven weeks the mother will start to demonstrate nesting behavior and starts to look for a place to give birth to her puppies. This might be her own basket or a special whelping box. This must be ready at least a week before the birth to give the mother time to get used to it. The basket or box should preferably be in a quiet place.

The birth

The average litter is between three and nine puppies. The birth usually passes without problems. Of course, you must contact your veterinarian immediately if you suspect a problem!

Suckling

After birth, the mother starts to produce milk. The suckling period is very demanding. During the first three to four weeks the pups rely entirely on their mother's milk. During this time she needs extra food and fluids. This can be up to three or four times the normal amount. If she's producing too little milk, you can give both mother and her young special puppy milk. Here too, divide the high quantity of food the mother needs over several smaller portions. Again, choose a concentrated, high-energy, food and give her plenty of fresh drinking water, but not cow's milk, which can cause diarrhea. You can give the puppies some supplemental solid food when they are three to four weeks old. There are special puppy foods available that follow on well from the mother's milk and can easily be eaten with their milk teeth.

Ideally, the puppies are fully weaned, at an age of six or seven weeks i.e. they no longer drink their mother's milk. The mother's milk production gradually stops and her food needs also drop. Within a couple of weeks after weaning, the mother should again be getting the same amount of food as before the pregnancy.

Castration and sterilization

As soon as you are sure your bitch should never bear a (new) litter, a sterilization is the best solution. During sterilization the uterus is removed in an operation. The bitch no longer goes into season

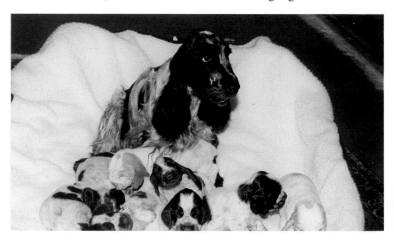

and can never become pregnant. The best age for a sterilization is about eighteen months, when the bitch is more or less fully-grown.

A male dog is usually only castrated for medical reasons or to correct undesirable sexual behavior. During a castration the testicles are removed, which is a simple procedure and usually without complications. There is no special age for castration but, where possible, wait until the dog is fully-grown. Vasectomy is sufficient where it's only a case of making the dog infertile. In this case the dog keeps its sexual drive but can no longer reproduce.
Castration and sterilization are often mentioned in the same breath as lethargy and obesity. Males and

females are no longer ruled by their reproduction hormones and can indeed become quieter. The change in the hormone household after the operation also means they have less need for energy. If you slightly adjust the amount of food your dog gets there need be no talk of obesity.

With Cocker bitches, changes in their coat structure appear in almost all cases following sterilization. Sometimes, the coat becomes very fuzzy and thus harder to care for. Changes in the coat can also occur with males following castration, but this problem almost never occurs after a vasectomy. Changes in the coat structure may be undesirable for show dogs.

Flyball

Sport and shows

English Cockers are active dogs that won't be satisfied with a quiet walk. They will soon get bored and will behave badly in the house. To keep your Cocker happy, you should do something together!

Sport

If you don't like the idea of hunt training, you can take part in other sports with your Cocker. But a Cocker Spaniel is, and will always be, a hunting dog with strong instincts.

Hunt training

For centuries, the Cocker Spaniel has been a fine hunting dog capable of penetrating thick cover (brambles, gorse etc.) where bigger dogs sometimes struggle. As a pet, it has kept the energy level of its hunting history. So a Cocker can happily use this energy during hunt training.

The breed association organises hunt-training courses, where various elements come into play. These include following on the lead, obeying whistle signals, retrieving over land and water, marking fallen game and searching and retrieving lost game in light and thick cover. It must also remain steady when gunshots are fired and must not pursue fleeing game.

At the end of the training season, the dog is tested to see if it's ready to take part in a so-called certification day. This day has an official character and at first seems to be a kind of competition. Your dog is given a number; there are judges and people walking around with shotguns. The judges assess things like the dog's willpower in the search in thin and thick cover, if it will retrieve on command (across water and land) and if will remain sitting on command and on shot.

The judge's assessment determines whether your dog qualifies for a certificate and, if so, for which certificate. The training certificate indicates how advanced you have got with training, the hunt certificate is awarded if your dog is considered suitable for hunting. Once you have that, you can register your dog in the young dog classification at the next field trials.

These trials are above all to test the way your dog works and faults are punished with penalty points, but still with a touch of affection. Then follow novice competitions (for dogs with less experience) and championship trials. Here, both dog and master are assessed in terms of how they work together. The combination should be as perfect as possible to qualify. For more information contact the breed association.

Agility

Agility is a form of dog sport where the dog, accompanied by its master, must run a certain course. On the way, various obstacles have to be mastered. The art is to do this as fast as possible with as few faults as possible. Agility competitions are organised by a large number of local dog clubs.

Flyball

Flyball is another form of dog sport. The dog must jump four fences and then press a plank with its paw. This launches a ball. The dog must then bring the ball to its master as fast as it can. Here too, the dog with the fastest time wins.

Exhibitions and exemption shows

Visiting a dog show is a pleasant experience for both dog and master, and for some dog-lovers it is an intensive hobby. They visit countless shows every year. Others find it nice to visit an exemption show with their dog just once. It's worth making the effort to visit an exemption show where a judge's experienced eyes will inspect your Cocker and assess it for form, gait, condition and behaviour. The judge's report will teach you your dog's weak and strong points, which may help you when chosing a mate for breeding. You can also exchange experiences with other Cocker owners. Official exemption shows are only open to dogs with a pedigree.

Ring training and club events

If you've never been to a dog show, you will probably be fumbling in the dark in terms of what will be expected of you and your dog. Many cocker and general dog clubs organise so-called ring training courses for dogs going to a show for the first time. This training teaches you exactly what the judge will be looking for, and you can practice this together with your dog.

Open shows

All dog clubs organise dog shows. You must enter your dog in advance in a certain class. These metings are usually small and friendly and are often the first acquaintance dog and master makes with a "real" judge. This is an overwhelming experience for your dog - a lot of its contemporaries and a strange man or woman who fiddles around with it and peers into its mouth. After a few times, your dog will know exactly what's expected of it and will happily go to the next club match.

Championship shows

Various championship shows take place during the course of the year with different prizes. These shows

are much more strictly organised than club matches. Your dog must be registered in a certain class in advance and it will then be listed in a catalogue. On the day itself, the dog is usually kept on a bench until its turn comes up. During the judging in the ring, it's important that you show your dog at its best. The judge examines each dog in turn. When all the dogs from that class have been judged, the best are selected and placed. After all the judging for is finished all the winners of the various classes in that sex they compete for the Challenge Certificate in that sex. (3 Challenge certificates from different judges, and your cocker will be a Champion in the UK.) The best Cocker in the eyes of the judge gets this award. Finally, the winners of each sex compete for the title of Best in Show.

Of course, your dog must look very smart for the show. The judge will not be impressed if its coat is not clean or is tangled, and its paws are dirty. Nails must be clipped and teeth free of plaque. The dog must also be free of parasites and ailments. A bitch must not be in season and a male must be in possession of both testicles. Apart from those things, judges also hate badly brought-up, anxi-

ous or nervous dogs. Get in touch with your local dog club or the breed association if you want to know more about shows.

Don't forget!

If you're planning to take your dog to a club match or in fact to any show, you need to be well prepared. Don't forget the following:

For yourself:
- Show documents if they have been sent to you
- Food and drink
- Clip for the catalogue number
- Chairs if an outside show

For your dog:
- Food and water bowls and food
- Dog blanket and perhaps a cushion
- Show lead
- A brush
- A benching chain and collar

What happens at a show?

Before the show, take your dog out for a little longer walk. A little 'accident' in the ring can always happen, but prevention is better. After you enter the hall, your dog must first go for a veterinary check. Vets check the dogs taking part for any infectious diseases. Bitches on heat are not permitted, neither are dogs without both testicles. You then have your qualification certificate stamped and

pick up your catalogue. You look for the cage with your number on it. These cages are only found at major shows. At club matches your dog can lie beside your seat. You may not change the allocation of cages to sit next to friends or acquaintances!

The catalogue shows in which ring judging will take place. Judging is in the sequence shown in the catalogue. You have to watch out yourself for your turn. Before judging starts, you give your qualification certificate to the ring official behind the desk in the ring. Then you give your dog a last brush and put its show lead on.

When it's time, you position yourself in the group at the ringside in the right order. Normally the judge will have the whole group walk a round or two. The dog should trot without pulling on the line. When the judge asks, you return to the ringside. Now follows individual judging.

The judge will ask you how old your dog is and ask you to show its teeth. He will then inspect the dog, sometimes from a distance and sometimes by touch. The judge will ask you to walk with your dog. After that, you sit your dog down nicely again and the judge will dictate his assessment to the secretary behind the desk in the ring. When the judge is finished, you go back to the end of the line so

that the next participant can show his or her dog. Once all dogs have been inspected, the judge will ask the whole group to stand up again and will make his choice and place the four best dogs.

Once all classes have been judged, the winners are judged against each other. The judge chooses the best dog (which is then the champion) and the vice-champion. Both dogs (male and bitch) are then judged against each other for the title "Best of Breed" This dog finally goes to the ring of honour.

In the ring, the judge is the boss and you must follow his instructions to the letter. Only the judge determines the result and there is no questioning that result. If there are irregularities, you can appeal to the ringmaster, who is responsible for what happens in the ring. Once the judge has signed the reports and qualification certificates, you can pick them up from the ring official. On showing these documents after the show, you can pick up any medal or prize you have won from the secretary.

Parasites

All dogs are vulnerable to various sorts of parasite. Parasites are tiny creatures that live at the expense of another animal. They feed on blood, skin and other body substances. There are two main types.

Internal parasites live within their host animal's body (tapeworm and round-worm) and external parasites live on the animals exterior, usually in its coat, fleas and ticks, but also in its ears (ear mite).

Fleas

Fleas feed on a dog's blood. They cause not only itching and skin problems, but can also carry infections such as tapeworm. In large numbers they can cause anaemia and dogs can also become allergic to a flea's saliva, which can cause serious skin conditions. So it's important to treat dog for fleas as effectively as possible, not just on the dog itself but also in its surroundings. For treatment on the animal, there are various medicines: drops for the neck and to put it in its food, flea collars, long-life sprays and flea powders. There are various sprays in pet shops that can be used to eradicate fleas in the dog's immediate surroundings. Choose a spray that kills both adult fleas and their larvae. If your dog goes in your car, you should spray that too. Fleas can also affect other pets, so you should treat those too. When spraying a room, cover any aquarium or fishbowl. If the spray reaches the water, it can be fatal for your fish!

Your vet and pet shop have a wide range of flea treatments and can advise you on the subject.

Ticks

Ticks are small, spider-like parasites. They feed on the blood of the animal or person they've settled on. A tick looks like a tiny, grey-

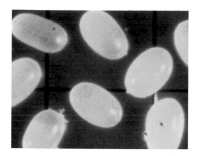

Flea-eggs

Fleas

coloured leather bag with eight feet. When it has sucked itself full, it can easily be five to ten times its own size and is darker in colour. Dogs usually fall victim to ticks in bushes, woods or long grass. Ticks cause not only irritation by their blood sucking but can also carry a number of serious diseases. This applies especially to the Mediterranean countries, which can be infested with blood parasites. In our country these diseases are fortunately less common. But Lymes disease, which can also affect humans, has reached our shores. Your vet can prescribe a special treatment if you're planning to take your dog to southern Europe. It is important to fight ticks as effectively as possible. Check your dog regularly, especially when its been running free in woods and bushes. It can also wear an anti-tick collar.

Removing a tick is simple using a tick pincette. Grip the tick with the pincette, as close to the dog's skin as possible and carefully pull it out. You can also grip the tick between your fingers and, using a turning movement, pull it carefully out. You must disinfect the spot where the tick was using iodine to prevent infection. Never soak the tick in alcohol, ether or oil. In a shock reaction the tick may discharge the infected contents of its stomach into the dog's skin.

Worms

Dogs can suffer from various types of worm, The most common are tapeworm and roundworm. Tapeworm causes diarrhoea and poor condition. With a tapeworm infection you can sometimes find small pieces of the worm around the dog's anus or on its bed. In this case, the dog must be wormed. You should also check your dog for fleas, which carry the tapeworm infection.

Roundworm is a condition that reoccurs regularly. Puppies are often infected by their mother's milk. Your vet has medicines to prevent this. Roundworm causes problems (particularly in younger dogs), such as diarrhoea, loss of weight and stagnated growth. In serious cases the pup becomes thin, but with a swollen belly. It may vomit and you can then see the worms in its vomit. They are spaghetti-like tendrils. A puppy must be treated regularly for worms with a worm treatment. Adult dogs should be treated every six months.

Ticks

Tapeworm

Roundworm

Your Cocker Spaniel's health

The space in this small book is too limited to go into all the medical ups and downs of the English Cocker Spaniel, but we do want to give you a little information about some conditions that affect this breed more than other dogs.

Breed-specific conditions

Sadly, the English Cocker Spaniel is not free of hereditary conditions. The breed is vulnerable to some eye ailments, and with the self-coloured, aggressiveness is sometimes a problem. The breed association and the breeders themselves try to wipe out these conditions by strict breeding policies.

Hip Dysplasia (HD)

The English Cocker is also a breed affected by hip dysplasia, albeit to a limited extent. The breed associations hope that strict monitoring of parent animals will keep it under control. They make examinations for HD mandatory for dogs bred by their members. By means of x-ray, dogs are checked for a (slight or serious) form of HD. If they are affected, they

may not be used for breeding.

Hip dysplasia is an anomaly in the rear hip joints whereby the hip socket does not properly enclose the head of the thigh bone. This causes infections and bone tumours that are extremely painful.

Until recently, it was assumed that HD was primarily caused by genetic factors. Recent investigations, however, indicate that while genetic factors certainly play a role in terms of a dog's susceptibility to HD, external factors such as food quality and exercise appear at least equally important. Limit the chance of HD as far as possible by giving your dog ready-made food of a good brand, and don't add any supplements! Make sure your dog doesn't get too fat.

A Cocker Spaniel pup should be protected from HD in its first year. Don't let it romp too much with other dogs or chase sticks and balls too wildly. These kinds of games cause the pup to make abrupt and risky movements, which can overburden its soft joints. One important but under-estimated factor that can course HD is the floor in your home. Parquet and tiled floors are much too slippery for a young dog. Regular slipping can cause com-plications that promote HD. If you have a smooth floor, it's advisable to lay blankets or old carpet in places the dog uses regularly. Let it spend lots of time in the garden as grass is a perfect surface to run on.

Progressive Retina Atrophy (PRA)

Progressive Retina Atrophy is an awful condition. Once it's found its way into a bloodline, PRA is difficult to eradicate. The disease is a progressive degeneration of the retina that inevitably leads to blindness. In the early stages, the dog will still be able to see well in daylight until it's about five years old, but between its fifth and ninth year the dog will become totally blind.

Cataracts

Checks for cataracts are made at the same time as the checks for PRA. Cataracts cause a clouding of the retina. The condition can occur in young animals and is passed on by both parents. If only a part of the retina is affected cataracts need not lead to total blindness, but unfortunately this is the consequence in most cases.

Breed Associations

Becoming a member of a breeder club can be very useful for good advice and interesting activities. Contact the Kennel Club in case addresses or telephonenumbers are changed.

The Kennel Club
1 Clarges Street
W1J 8AB
London UK
Tel: 0870 606 6750
Website: http://www.the-kennel-club.org.uk

Cocker Spaniel Club
Sec. Mrs A Webster
Tel: 01530 249952
Email: Anne@Thecockerspaniel club.Co.Uk
www.thecockerspanielclub.co.uk

Cocker Spaniel Club Of Scotland
Sec. Mrs Wilma Reid
Tel: 01555 870373
www.cockerspanielclubScot.Fsnet.co.uk
Email: Wilma.Reid@btinternet.com

Cheshire Cocker Spaniel Club
Sec. Miss D Stonier
Tel: 01625 424343

Cocker Spaniel Club Of Lancashire
Sec. Mrs Grice
Tel: 01744 605581

Coventry Cocker Spaniel Club
Sec. Mrs L Parker
Tel: 01908 565088

Devon & Cornwall Cocker Spaniel Club
Sec. Miss S Ellison
Tel: 01884 881 449

East Anglian Cocker Spaniel Society
Sec. Mrs Sawko, Tel: 01480 212459

**East Of Scotland
Cocker Spaniel Club**
Sec. Mrs M Hynd
Tel: 01383 881967

**Hampshire & Sussex
Cocker Spaniel Club**
Sec. Mrs P A Morton
Tel: 01256 862747

**Home Counties Cocker
Spaniel Club**
Sec. Mrs S Sadler
Tel: 01206 213680

**London Cocker
Spaniel Society**
Sec. Anne Moore
Email: Lcss24@hotmail.com

**Midland Cocker
Spaniel Club**
Sec. Mr R M A Pain
Tel: 0121 453 3215

**North Midlands & Eastern
Counties Cocker Spaniel Club**
Sec. Mrs J Pretty
tel : 01283 820867

**North Of England Cocker
Spaniel Assoc**
Sec. Mr Hall
Tel: 01925 226059

**North Of Ireland Cocker
Spaniel Club**
Sec. Mr J Mcdowell
Tel: 01960 367659

**North Wales Cocker
Spaniel Club**
Sec. Miss A Hughes
Tel: 01745 353715

**Parti-Coloured Cocker
Spaniel Club**
Sec. Mrs Steeples
Tel: 01530 244260

**Rotherham & District
Cocker Spaniel Club**
Sec. Mr A Curry
Tel: 01757 708105

**Solid Colours Cocker
Spaniel Assoc**
Sec. Miss S Kettle
Tel: 01268 554619

**South Wales &
Monmouthshire
Cocker Spaniel Club**
Sec. Mrs J M Craig
Tel: 01792 864402

Ulster Cocker Spaniel Club
Sec. Mr J Mcdowell
Tel: 01960 367659

**West Of England
Cocker Spaniel Club**
Sec. Mr D Shapland
Tel: 01793 751102
www.westofenglandcocker
club.co.uk

**Yorkshire Cocker
Spaniel Club**
Sec. Mr D Shields
Tel: 01751 473620

Tips for the Cocker Spaniel

- Don't let your puppy romp with bigger, heavy dogs

- Don't only fight fleas, but their larvae too.

- Make sure your dog doesn't get too fat. Not too much to eat and plenty of exercise is the golden rule.

- Follow a puppy course with your dog. You'll both benefit.

- A puppy means a lot of work and sometimes a few grey hairs.

- A Cocker Spaniel has a beautiful, but time-consuming coat.

- Buy a Cocker Spaniel via the breed association.

- Never buy a puppy if you weren't able to see its mother.

- Visit several breeders before you buy a puppy.

- A Cocker Spaniel will be quiet in the home if it can work off its energy running free.

- Single-coloured (Self) Cockers normally need a stricter, more rigorous up-bringing than variegated dogs.

- Make your puppy's first car journey a pleasant experience. A dog that doesn't like travelling in a car can cause a lot of problems.

- Taking your dog with you on holiday? Why not?

The Cocker Spaniel

Official name:	English Cocker Spaniel
FCI-classification:	Group 8 Hunting Dogs
First standard:	1902 (England)
Origin:	England
Original tasks:	Hunting dog
Shoulder height:	Males: 39-41 cm (15.5-16 inches)
	Bitches: 38-39 cm (15-15.5 inches)
Weight:	12.7-14.5 kg (28-32 lbs.)
Average life expectancy:	12-13 years

the **Cocker Spaniel**